First Published 2024

Corksail Books

KDP ISBN 9798327761476

Text Eileen D'Gama

Illustrations Eileen D'Gama

All rights reserved

Corksail Books

Aliens in the Mars Yard

Teeny tiny aliens called Roo and Pip were floating around in space and surfing on the solar winds.

They surfed next to a spacecraft which was examining the sun and skidded down it's solar arrays like a skateboarder grinding down a rail.

Even though they were normally quite small, Roo and Pip had a special shrink-grow gun which they could use to change size and become even smaller.

One day they made themselves so small that the astronauts on the I.S.S. (International Space Station) didn't even notice when they floated inside after a spacewalk.

The next morning
astronaut Tim Peake was doing his weightless
exercises of somersaults and star-stretches. Roo and Pip
decided to join in. They giggled and laughed as Tim
stretched out his fingers and toes.

But as they tumbled in a very impressive 3 somersaults in a row, they got too near to Tim and bumped against his ear.

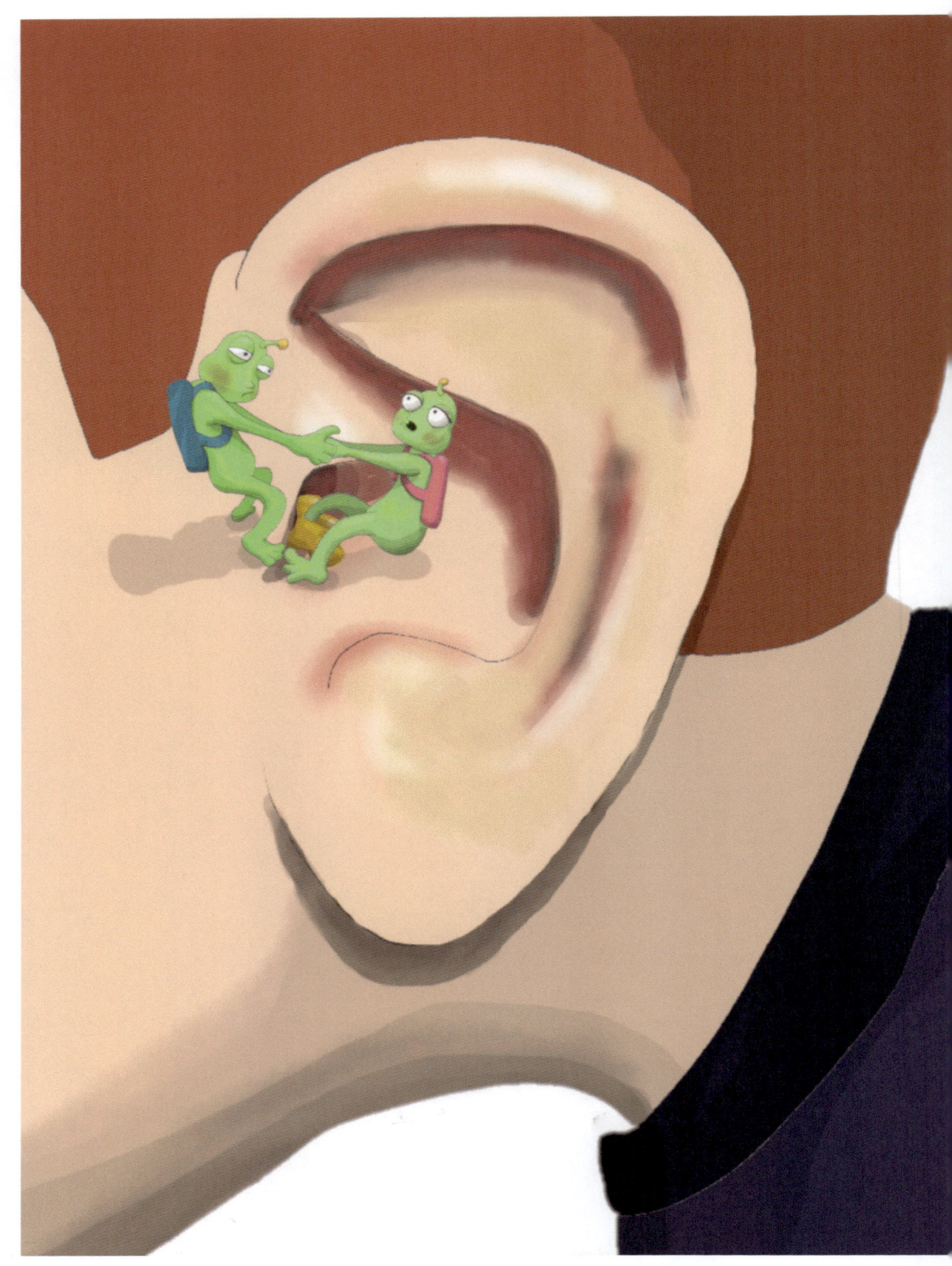

Pip accidentally put her foot in some yellow sticky stuff and when Roo tried to help her out, he got stuck in it too. Earwax really is very sticky!

International Space Station

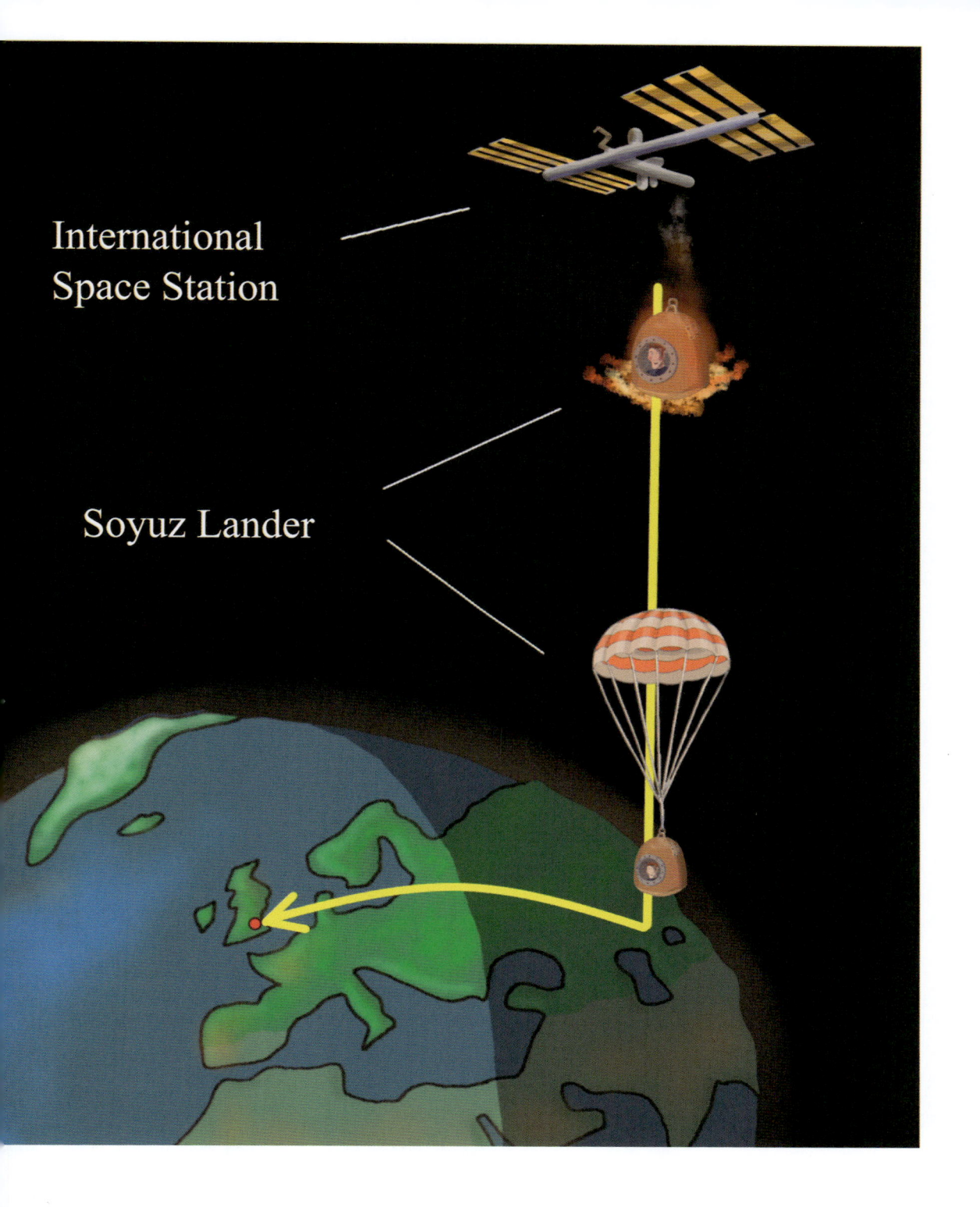

Soyuz Lander

A couple of weeks later, after Tim Peake had landed safely back on earth, he made a visit to Airbus at Stevenage where they design and make space satellites.

The tour took him
to a low rectangular building
with a room called the Mars Yard,
which is full of red coloured sand and angular rocks and
looks just like the surface of Mars. Tim tested a big
remote-controlled vehicle called the Mars Rover.

Suddenly Tim felt an itch in his ear. As he scratched it the little aliens Roo and Pip tumbled down through the air and landed on the Martian-like surface next to a lump of wax.

They would be quite safe in here as the Mars Rover which drives about is SO SLOW that there is no chance of being run over.

One day they noticed it was very noisy. The air was filled with lots of chatter of excited children and grown-ups coming in and out for the Airbus Family Fun Day. This was very unusual, so they decided to investigate.

Hidden behind a large rock,
Roo and Pip used the shrink-grow gun to make themselves about the same size as the human children.

Just as the tour guide got to the bit where he chuckled and said *'Of course, there are no aliens in our Mars Yard'*, Roo and Pip stepped out from behind their rock.

Everyone laughed as they thought it was part of the show. The people did not realise that they were real aliens and just thought that they were children in fabulous costumes.

They left their sandy home and popped next-door into the STEM Discovery centre. It was so much fun! There were experiments about magnetism, light, and lots of other cool things. Roo made lightening from his fingers and Pip made forces with dangling magnets.

When they left the building there were more new things to try. The little aliens had a go at riding the Twirly Teacups which felt like being in their Martian saucer-cars.

The bouncy slide reminded them of jumping on their marshmallow moon called Phobos. There, gravity is different to Earth. So sometimes on Phobos they would jump so high that they didn't even come back down.

In VR museum they could see all of the planets in the middle of the room. The virtual planets were huge and beautiful, and it made Roo "beep" with excitement. *That's our planet* he said pointing with his headset on. The man nearby thought he was pointing at Earth but really, he was pointing at Mars, the 4th planet from the sun.

Just around a corner, they came across an enormous towering robot. At first he seemed a bit scary but he was really quite funny and soon they were dancing around with him.

'*That was amazing*' Roo said to Pip '*but I'm a bit tired now. Can we get an ice cream and then sneak back to the Mars Yard for a nap?*' On the way back, they wandered through the main building looking at space satellites being made.

There were panels made of honeycomb (no, not made by bees!) which were surprisingly light to hold. These were used to build the shiny, mirrored satellite walls.

They saw special pipes called heatpipes that moved heat so quickly that if you put one end in hot coffee, the other end would feel hot straight away. Best to use a teaspoon!

When they arrived back at the Mars Yard, they were happy and tired. Pip shrank them both back down to tiny size. It felt just like being back on their home planet Mars. Home sweet home and nobody would ever realise that they were there.

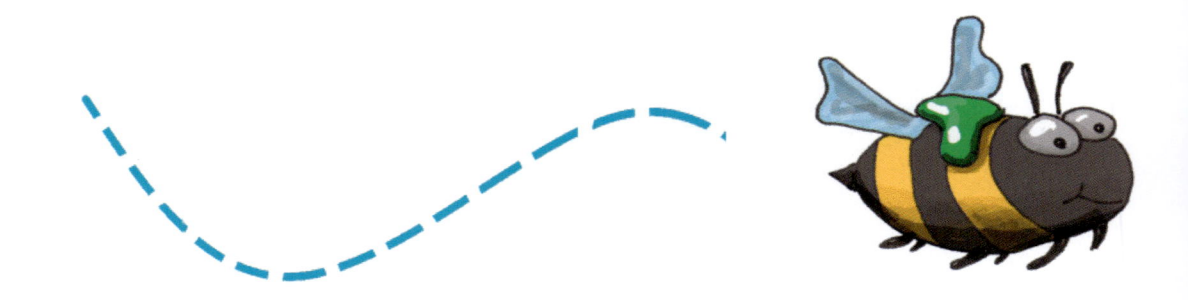

THE END

Many many thanks to Tim Peake for not objecting to this story – or my portrayal of him! Tim has created some brilliant books for children of his own which include the action-filled adventures *Swarm Rising* and *Swarm Enemy* (with Steve Cole) and, for anyone who wants to find out more about space and loves lots of facts, there's *The Cosmic Diary of Our Incredible Universe* and *The Cosmic Diary of a Future Space Explorer* (all published by Hachette Children's Books).

Look out for more stories illustrated by Eileen D'Gama:
Angus The Little White Fluffy Cloud Who Fell In Love With The Sun.
Gordon the Little Ghost Who Was Very Bored.
Travis The Little Tractor Who Couldn't Stop Laughing.
Mrs Marmalade and the Goblin who stole the toys.
Available on Amazon. (Did you spot some of them in this book?)

Printed in Great Britain
by Amazon